FROM LOSER
TO WINNER

FROM LOSER TO WINNER

30 SECRETS OF LEADING
A VICTORIOUS LIFE.

SAMINA SAIFEE

PARTRIDGE
A Penguin Random House Company

To order additional copies of this book, contact
Partridge India
000 800 10062 62
orders.india@partridgepublishing.com

www.partridgepublishing.com/india

Contents

Dedication

FATHER:
SHABBIR SHAMSHUDDIN SAIFEE.

MOTHER:
BILKIS SHABBIR SAIFEE.

THE AUTHOR DECLARES THE CREDIT FOR HER PASSIONATE WRITING WHICH WAS DISCOVERED WAS THROUGH HER SPECIAL FRIEND, JOAN RODRIGUES.

SHE IS THANKFUL TO HER DEAR ONE MUSTAFA (NAUSHAD) KHUMRI FOR HIS HARD EFFORTS TO MAKE THIS BOOK A GREAT SUCCESS.

Acknowledgements

Here's a confession:

A heartfelt thanks to all the assistants and participants who made these dream come true. Your inspiring heroic efforts and your courage in confronting the obstacles and ordeals helped me to make these a great outcome.

The book you hold in your hands has been published into its present shape by the Publishing Consultant Maveric Pana who prompted me with this idea to issue it successfully. We have never met but our way of interacting through phone and through exchange of emails almost makes me feel the sense of genuine human touch.

I'd like to thank my dear one Naushad (Mustafa) Khumri who ultimately made this publishing workout through his great effort and made sure that this book reaches to every reader all over the world.

Thank you, for being who you truly are as a role model for the vision of this great book that the world so desperately needs.

I am thankful to God for blessing me with this book to get published and issued and to every reader who has this book in their hands.

WHO IS A LEADER?

Leadership is a process by which a person influences others to accomplish an objective and directs the organization in a way that makes it more cohesive and coherent. Although leaders have the authoritative power of leadership this power can't make you a leader, it simply makes you a boss. Leadership differs in that. It makes the followers want to achieve high goals rather than simply bossing around and slave-driving people.

You are a leader of your own life as you tend to feel it in your own way. But those people who prove to excel themselves in such a way that they also make others leading them as their followers are the real leaders. So a leader is the hero of our dramatic life experience where the scene is to create himself as a great hero performing on the stage and his followers are his great fans who ape and follow whatever he does to act. Playing the role of a great leader is a one-man show. The tickets charged to watch his show performance is nothing more than a loud round of applause as an appreciation to showcase the scene of the show in public who will follow them.

For instance: The king of pop, Michael Jackson, leaded a heroic life by almost casting a spell on his fans with his stunt performance. Though he is no more, his music inspires many people who are his followers all over the world.

"He who gains a victory over men is strong, but, he who gains a victory over himself is all powerful"

- By Chinese Philosopher, Lao Taze.

Who Is A Leader?

I am a leader

I am a hero of my life

If I believe in myself

I can change this world

To suit other's life,

I can move mountains

With my faith

I can reach

The height of sky

With my fate,

I am here to lead

I am here not to sow

A follower's seed.

THE UNIVERSAL LAW OF BONDING.

Man alone is the architect of his own destiny. Give the world your best and the best will come back to you. The greatest gift you can give anyone is your realization of your own personal growth.

The universal law of bonding is, "I cry, You cry", "I cherish, You cherish".

These are the vibes we get from each other as we are in a vicious social circle. The positive vibes will make a person optimistic in every way, whereas negative vibes spreads pessimism among us. The negativity deteriorates your progress and makes the world around you to turn apart. If you are able to recognize your thoughts, leading yourself to an action, be it positive or negative, you will be able to work on your mental analysis. The universal law of bonding between human beings is a chain reaction. This chain sustains the universal presence of your social existence.

"Realize one important truth of the universe that everything is connected to everything in some way".

-Leonardo De Vince

The universal law of bonding:

For emotional bond to prevail

Humanity is never curtailed,

In order to keep universe bonded

We stay spiritually united,

It is a strong string of thread

Where if one is lost

Others suffer almost,

The law of bonding is as such

We care for our emotions so much.

DESIRE: YOUR LONGING FOR IT.

According to Napoleon Hill, an American author, "Desire is the starting point of all achievements."

Desire is the fuel in the furnace of your life time.

A person with a burning desire to achieve any kind of goal is automatically driven towards it.

It is said "Where there is a will, there is a way".

Nothing could be as strong as your power of willingness.

Make a wish and you shall have it come true if you persistently strive for it.

Desire shapes your dream.

Your willpower towards your goal sets you free from the world's most impossible things.

For instance: George Bernard Shaw, an irish playwright, socialist and a co-founder of the London school of Economics, wanted to publish his piece of writing but for 9 years every publisher turned him down. Bernard Shaw persisted through the tough times and kept writing, kept submitting his work, and kept on believing in his dreams. Year after year as the time passed by, he kept on writing passionately and he got better and better at it until ultimately he succeeded inevitably. His first manuscript which got published became popular and he became one of the most celebrated Author in history.

Your desire should be to such an extent that your inner voice whisers to you "Do or Die".

Don't forgo your burning desire.

"Life is a series of collisions with the future. It is not the sum of what we have but what we yearn to be."

-lose Ortega

Desire-Your longing for it:

I longed for something I desire

I thought it was so higher,

It was such a passion

To be a person of success,

That I moved on

With every single thought

Without any quest.

THE POWER OF IMAGINATION

What you visualize you realize. Your imagination shapes you. You cannot be robbed off from the unique gift meant for you and that gift is your dream or your imagination. No one can kill your dream except you. You need to execute your dream. Napoleon Bonaparte, a French military and political leader, says "Imagination rules the world". The only asset you possess in this materialistic world in reality is your imagination. The power of imagination makes you to have your broad sense. Imagine yourself and it will drive you to reality. Set your mind free from limited thoughts. Expand your power of Imagination. Albert Einstein, a German-born theoretical physicist, mathematician and a philosopher of science said "Imagination is more important than knowledge". The more you expand the boundaries of your imagination, opening up new territories and going beyond what you think is possible, more doors of opportunities will be unlocked for you leading you to the most extraordinary space of the world to see. The greatest gift of imagination power for us is that it has no limits and it crosses the border of your thinking without refraining you from your power to imagine.

"There Is a law in psychology that says if you form a picture in your imagination of what you would like to be, and you keep and hold that picture there long enough, you will soon become exactly as you have been thinking".

-William James.

The power of imagination:

I have a power

To Imagine

What I am,

Sometimes I am this

Sometimes I am that,

My mere imagination

Brings me to realization,

That I can be real

For what I need to be

In this make-believe world.

YOUR STRUGGLING PERIOD
FOR SUCCESS.

In the era of survival-of-the-fittest, we need to struggle for us to succeed as a social being. The person who goes ahead and strives hard to achieve success has to undergo every possible peril practically. A successful person normally tends to get success with optimistic mindset, pragmatically being oblivious of pessimism in his progressive life.

As a leader you have to face many difficulties and different phases of life. The battle is your very own life landing you towards the war between success and failure. If you want to win by fighting the situation you need not fly, but incase you fly from it then you have given up the fact to face the reality that you are a great success.

"Success seems to be connected with action, Successful people keep moving. They make mistakes, but don't Quit"

- Conrad Hilton, of the Hilton Hotel Empire.

Your struggling period for success:

In the middle of the journey

I left my destiny

For struggling was destined

And success was mine,

If I keep running

The right path

My efforts will pay

With other roads

Which are stoned

Setting it apart.

FEAR AS YOUR FRIEND.

The greatest enemy of your success, the greatest hindrance to your success and to become everything you are capable of becoming, is and always will be fear. Try to do things you think you cannot do.

Samuel Langhorne Clemens known by his pen name Mark Twain who was an American author and humorist once wrote "Courage is not the lack of fear, absence of fear. It is the control of fear, mastery of fear". The universe has abounded good gifts of natural bounties bestowed upon you demonstrating courage. It is you who fail to recognize it and stay fearful. Ralph Waldo Emerson, an American essayist, lecturer, and poet said "Do the thing you fear and the death of fear is certain".

The actor, Grand Ford once said, "If you do not do the thing you fear, the fear will control your life".

Fear makes you go through poor plight of poor power which can almost paralyze you. Face the fact, Face the fear. "A good coward dies a thousand deaths, a hero dies but once." Forgo the fear and follow your dreams. David Viscott, the noted psychiatrist says "Everyone has a life sentence". Each of us are destined to great successful life without fear in our mind.

"The purpose of life after all is to live it, to taste the experience to the utmost, to reach out eagerly without fear for newer or richer experiences."

—*Eleanor Roosevelt.*

Fear as your friend:

Fear sees stumbling blocks

Fear sees stepping-stones!

Fear makes you dreadful in the end

To get what you dreamt of

In this honourable land.

YOU ARE ACCOUNTABLE TO ACT.

Embrace the reality that you are incharge of your very own life. No one except you can make yourself succeed or make you fail. The greatest deterrent factor towards life is the victim's mentality. When you try to blame others, you make them your victim. Don't be a victim, be a volunteer. Nothing destroys your goal or your purpose to serve your satisfying life. Responsibility means to respond with ability to act rather than react. Remind yourself that you are responsible foryour life and not others. Stop thinking and start acting as action speaks more than words. You need not play a Blame-Game. Speak to your inner-voice with the wake of your conscious mind saying, "I am responsible".

"When things are handed to you, you lose that burning edge to prove to the world that you are outstanding".

-Dr. Joyce Brothers.

You Are Accountable To Act:

Do not rely

On other's decision

Be achiever of

Your own real action,

You are accountable indeed

Of your own action and deed,

Do not get mislead,

Account yourself to sow

A successful seed

For sweet fruits

Of results to reap!

REACHING THE DESTINY AS A LEADER.

A leader is a person who lives life rather than spends his life. Now the major distinction between living life and spending it is that the formal makes you fruitful in every aspect while you live whereas later one which you lead makes you to stay the way as it is going without any concern for where you want to lead yourself for your much awaited destiny. A leader is a person who will not blame fate for his failure but will have faith by changing his destiny by reaching at a successful venture in his future life.

Helen Keller, an American author, political activist, and lecturer said, "Life is either a daring adventure or nothing."

Remember, it is a choice not a chance that determines your destiny.

"Destiny is not the matter of chance, it is a matter of choice. It is not a thing to be waited for, it is a thing to be achieved."

-William Bryan.

Reaching The Destiny As A Leader:

Bereft of what is destined

We craved for every thing

Saying," its mine",

Like a rat in the race

We follow each other

At every phase,

What if one excels and

Wins the race?

So lead the life

Do not follow,

If you follow

You may not win

You may lose

If you are not keen.

SKY IS THE LIMIT.

Erma Bombeck, an American humourist, journalist, and columnist once said "Life and liberty are a piece of cake compared to the pursuit of happiness". For you to achieve an eternal success you need to limit your liberty and free yourself from the sense of failure. No one fails if they have the innermost faith to fly like a free bird in the firmament of borderless sky. Focus on the future plans and set it accordingly. Remember, there is no border line for you to cross the limits of your success. When you stare blankly at the sky where stars sparkle infinitely, you may realize the law of nature where your future is bright like those shining stars enveloped on the farthest sky. You are a shining star starring in the movie of world's dramatic life. Success comes to you when you try to achieve and makes you reach the heights of faded sky where you perish.

"Dare to live the life you have dreamed for yourself."

-Ralph Waldo Emerson.

Sky Is The Limit:

Follow your heart

Set yourself free,

Shine as bright as star

For the world to see,

Sky is the limit

For your future

To hold you

In a minute,

Fly free

Float on the cloud

Get your mind lighter

Fly and float higher,

With that borderless sky

You are apart from world

Setting yourself high,

So try, try and try

Do not give up

Until you die

When merged

With the blue sky!

YOUR ATTITUDE CARRIES YOU.

Whenever you ask yourself the mysterious question, Who am I? Your mirror image reflects to you directly with the universal answer which is quite undeniably evasive. When the question arises that, Am I existing in the presence of imagery world? Your self image lies to you, "I am, What I am?". You are the product of your own experiences and the victim of your own circumstances.

The world's biggest lie is when you are not being true to yourself.

When you portray a false pretence, being a hypocrite, you lose your real image. You are what you think. Do not get dettered due to the attitude you carry for yourself. Do not let your mind rule over you but you rule your mind.

"Human being can alter their lives by altering their attitude of mind"
—*Dr. William James.*

Your Attitude Carries You:

Optimism is a treasure

Pessimism has no measure

Be positive

Change your attitude

Wearing a good mindset

Its all within you to get,

Your attitude carries you

It can not be a Make-believe.

THE MAKING OF A LEADER.

Can leadership be learned? Good leaders are made not born. If you have a desire and willpower, you can become an effective leader. Good leaders develop through a never ending process of self-study, education, training and experience.

The making of a leader incorporates the very fact that every time you make mistakes you get a lesson to learn yourself. The unlocking of success key lies in knowing what makes you a leader. You are designed to achieve, you are engineered for success, you are endowed with the seeds of it. What do leaders do which makes them a leader? Leadership can be learned. It is something more than leading. Webster's dictionary defines leadership as the "Ability to lead".

All leaders possess cetain traits like:

Integrity, knowledge, courage, decisiveness, initiative, tact, justice, enthusiasum, endurance, loyalty and judgement. These traits leaves you nowhere but in the making of a leader for you.

"Nature magically suits a man his fortune, by making them the fruit of his character."

-Ralph Waldo Emerson.

The Making Of A Leader:

Lead the leader's life

Set the slave within you

Apart to oblige

Who is a leader of yourself,

When the slave within you

Answers itself?

Saying...

"I am great"

To be a leader

I won't regret.

LEADERSHIP TRAITS.

Ralph Waldo Emerson, an American essayist, lecturer, and poet says, "Do not go where path may lead, go instead where there is no path and leave a trail".

The traits of leadership lies in many ways. The skills to be a leader is acquired or inborn. The person who has extraordinary quality of dealing with people or confronting crisis is the one who is known to set leadership traits within him. The first and foremost quality that these leaders have is that they don't just follow but they think daringly different than others.

Good leaders are consistently working and studying to consolidate their leadership skills; they are not resting on their laurels.

You are a leader of your life.

All you need is to put forth the leader which lies within you. What do we possess for being a good leader? It comprises of being confident, being kind and firm, to be an expert, be decisive, be willing to face the criticism or crisis, manage time appropriately, have a vision, have concern for people you lead and mentor people.

The bottom line is that those who find themselves in leadership, bestowed upon them as a natural birthright or as an acquired skill or simply by accident must manifest certain leadership skills if they hope to succeed.

"Every man has consumate genius within him, some appear to have it more than others only because they are more aware of it than others are and the awareness and unawareness of it is what transforms each one of them into masters or holds them down to mediocrity."

-By Author, Warren Russell.

Leadership Traits:

I have some quality

Which is so distinct

With no equality,

I would lead myself

To win the cup

At first

And shall never

Kiss the dust.

HOW TO WIN OVER YOUR CREDIBILITY.

You are a great success if you shoulder the responsibilities of your life. The credit of your success goes to you indeed. The moment you were born you celebrated the wonderful event of humanly life and to make it a remarkable success. All you need to do is follow yourself and not others who will lead you. Be a leader not a follower. Practice rather than preach. Create your own self-identity placed in a dignified manner. Do not bring disgrace to your image by seeing others in your mirror. Do not pass the buck when you lose something in life but take onus of what you lost. You are the winner of your own success as a leader. The credit goes to you ultimately. So cherish the moment as a successful leader rather than a poor follower who follows his own dark shadow wandering adrift for achieving success as a leader in the light of his life being deprived of lime-light.

"No man has a chance to enjoy permanent success until he begins to look in the mirror for the real cause of his mistakes."

—*Napoleon Hill.*

How To Win Over Your Credibility:

I credited my success

To my work at first

And then came

The destiny

To salute it at last,

My success

Is credibly strong

If my efforts

Are not highly wrong,

To blame it on fate

When we fail it is unfair

To nature's judgement

If our faith isn't clear

To make achievement

IMAGINATION:
THE POWER TO MAKE IT REAL.

What is reality and What is an imagination? Is it a real imagination? Is your imagination out of your perception? Is your perception the real solution out of reality? Let's conclude the real solution that what you imagine in life, it can take the shape of reality for you. If your perception is not real you will fail to imagine the reality of life. It raises a brain-storming and thrilling question in your mind where curiosity kills you more and more until you don't discover the real answer for your life. Psychologically the image you carry within yourself sets you to make it real. The great power of imagination makes you clear in vision and then the reality sets back. When you imagine to make an initiative towards your action itself, you get mentally prepared to take things into action and those actions transforms you to the reality of life. The power of imagination is the greatest treasure which lies within you and no one can claim its reality from you at all.

"I know for sure that what we dwell on is who we become".

-Oprah Winfrey.

Imagination:
The Power To Make It Real:

I imagined myself

In front of mirror

But not found yet who am I?

I care if my image is really

The way I look

Or else I may be imagery,

To gain the power

To imagine what I want to be

It is my real imagination

Drawn to me.

THE JOURNEY OF MOVING TOWARDS SUCCESS.

The journey of moving your life towards success can make you face many barriers. It will make you go through the fact of being a failure, the duration of period which says to you, "You are a loser". As a loser your life will make a turning point at any time if you struggle, striving hard to succeed, winning the battle and gaining victory over the adventurous life. Life is an expedition where you discover new things every now and then. For a loser it serves as an opportunity to win over an obstacle he faces. Now, the vexed question lies is that "Can a loser be a leader?" To define a loser in general terms would mean the person who stays unhappy and unsatisfied with what life has offered him and at the same time cannot have the vision to see what luck has in store for him.

Rainer Maria Rilke, a Bohemian-Austrian poet and novelist says, "The only journey is the one within".

There are no accidents in the universe despite that most people believe in it. Realize that everything that befalls you, may be good or bad is a result of some action in the past however distant. The definition of serendipity in the Oxford concise dictionary is "the making of fortunate discoveries by seeming accident." The serendipity principle will only kick in when you are absolutely confident and it will all work out for your highest good. Every part of your life is exactly as it should be. Do not wait for perfect conditions. If every mother waited for perfect conditions before getting pregnant none of us would be here.

"Many of life's failures are people who did not realize how close they were to success when they gave up."

-Thomas Edison

The Journey Of Moving Towards Success:

Success is a journey

To reach you at top,

Success is not a destiny

Where you stop,

What you want to achieve

In a spur of moment

In a span of time

You may receive,

It is a journey

Of wandering

Here and there adrift

Till you don't get a lift,

Invest your hopes

In full faith

Till you do not achieve it

Do not give up or sit back!

SECRET OF SUCCESS.

Everyone in this world are successful provided they face to figure it out. Every one of us have a talent and we are all talented people in different ways. For instance, an Indian Artist Aamir Khan of Bollywood industry who achieved stardom, made a remarkable success through his show "Satyamav Jayate" to create awareness among Indian people by transforming entire society. He portrayed the ugly Indian image in order to serve a noble cause being benevolent for the betterment of society.

When you reveal the secret of your success within you, you will notice that it was your optimism, capability to deal with ordeals in your life, your perception towards the world, your own attitude and above all your persistence towards it. The formula for the key to success is "Don't give up until you don't get success".

Abraham Maslow, the noted psychiatrist said, "The story of the human race is the story of men and women selling themselves short".

Persistence means staying on your course regardless of obstacles, opposition, discouragement, distressment, and being deterrent. Persistence or perseverance are the most important qualities of success. Your persistence is really the true measure of your belief in yourself.

The secret gets unveiled when you reveal yourself, your integrity or elements which contributes to your success in life.

"Effort only fully releases its reward after a person refuses to quit."
-Napoleon Hill.

Secret Of Success:

My key to success

Was my failure itself,

My secret of answer

Was in question itself,

When asked about

My secret of success

I said," success is my journey

Not a destiny",

With adventures to follow

With challenges to call upon

It is a path that

Moves me on.

WHO IS A LOSER?

When you lose something during the struggling period of your life, you tend to presume that life does not give you a chance to be a successful person. We normally leave our issues to fate rather than having faith. The power of belief creates a world around you when you believe in yourself first. Do not focus on what is missing out in your life. It will make you feel there is a vaccum in it. Transcend the challenges you take and face the responsibility on your shoulders.

Napoleon Hill quoted that "Whatever the mind of man can conceive and believe it can achieve".

The world's greatest matter of fact is that you lose nothing but seeing other's gaining their success you feel the pain of being a loser. Instead of drawing attention or having careful observation what life has in store for you, you tend to crave for those things you cannot achieve. This inferior complexion inbuilt in you makes you see yourself as a loser in life. In essence loser is a person who has given up his dreams, remains rigid, and doesn't keeps his mind open to accept changes. If you scrutinize your failure and set forth yourself from loosing yourself as a loser and leading yourself as a leader within you, you have learned to manage the "Heroism" within you.

For instance, BIG B[Amitabh Bacchan] of Bollywood industry has proved himself far more successful as an Artist rather than in any other field of his prospective career, because he was able to discover the right channnel of his career where his real inbuilt talent lies.

As every human in this world has a talent; if he discovers his talent within him, he enters the right track riding him to the right path of success as a Winner.

"If you have any talent and don't use it you've failed".

-Thomas Wolfe.

43

Who Is A Loser?

The person unfortunate

May be termed as loser in this world

But action speaks more than any words,

Nothing much to lose

Nothing much to gain

No one knows how to make them

Defense with winner's aim,

Life is a secured gift

Wrapped for those

Who care for it,

For loser

It is to lose

Being something worth,

For winner

It is surely

Great invention

On earth.

SECRET OF HAPPINESS.

Happiness is a key which leads you to a successful life. What makes you feel happy? It is the innermost feeling which makes you feel good in your life. Some people aren't aware why they remain unhappy and so they fail to resolve issues by which they are upset. The secret of being happy lies within you when you discover true reasons of what makes you cherish and be delightful. Happiness is not in getting but it is in being and becoming. Anyone can be happy.

Extensive research has shown that people who remain happy prove to be more kind and caring, going out of their way in helping others. They are more loving, forgiving and even more creative than unhappy people. Happiness is a psychological phenomena. It spreads to other people around you only if you are happy too. You will never become excellent at something unless you are happy and you love doing it out of your passion.

Mark Twain said, "Make your vocation your vacation and your vacation your vocation". Very few people in this world can master anything. Have the courage and passion to do what you want to do and master it. Do like Napoleon Hill said "I see only the objective. The obstacle must give way". Be what nature intended for you and you will happily succeed. Whenever you feel unhappy as askew in your life, stop and ask yourself, "what is it in my life that I am not facing and dealing with?". It could be holding grudge on someone, or getting inferiority complex, looking down on others, by repressing it into the subconscious, it causes us to feel askew with our life. When a person resigns in life to an unfulfilling situation that does not bring them peace and makes him self-contented, they are extremely deprived of happiness in life.

"The way to have a happy life is to be busy doing what you like all the time, having no time left for you to consider whether you are happy or not".

-Bernard Shaw.

Secret Of Happiness:

Happiness is created by us

No matter what we do

To achieve it at any cost,

If we feel gloomy in our days

It is due to our own mindset,

The secret lies in you!

To remain happy

With your own perception

It is a secret affair

Carrying a candid conception.

FAILURE: THE LEARNING LESSON OF LIFE.

To achieve success in your life, it is good to accept failure. Failure doesn't mean you are a fool, but it means you still need to learn more lessons of wisdom. Failure doesn't mean closing the door of success but it means struggling or searching to get the real key for it. Life is a biggest lesson and you are a perpetual student, every chapter opens your mind with a new subject, even if you fail these subjects, you stand chances of learning more and more.

So, as the cliche' goes "Failure is a stepping stone to success." We may add further that...." Don't fall while stepping on those stones". You need not kiss the dust but be victorious.

Measure your failures and treasure your success.

"Failure is a great teacher, if you're open to it"

-Oprah Winfrey.

Failure: The Learning Lesson of Life.

We got a talent

Which is our treasure

To show it to world

Is our pleasure,

Do not fail pessimistically

Opt to win optimistically,

Life is a lesson to learn

When you do not

Put your fingers

In a furnace to burn.

HOW TO SET GOALS?

The great Chinese philosopher, Confucius says, "Man who shoots at nothing may hit it."

If you need to set goals, you should have a clear vision of aiming at the success you want to achieve. The fear to face the future can hinder your path to set goals in your life. You should know and have awarenesss about what you want to do in the wake of your conscious mind. Remember not to wander adrift in your path of success. Map the road of your destination where you want to go. Choose the way for it. Goal setting gives you a chance to choose your great fortune greeting you with great future to go ahead.

Denis Watley, an author, writes "Most people spend there time in tension relieving activities rather than goal achieving activities getting no closer to the goals they haven't even set for themselves".

If you don't know where to lead yourself, no road will take you there. The Holy book of Bible states, "Where there is no vision the people perish". Malcolm Stevenson Forbes, a publisher of Forbes Magazine stated that "When you cease to dream, you cease to live." Goal setting is a master skill of success.

"The world makes way for the man who knows where he's going."
                                                                  -Ralph Waldo Emerson.

How To Set Goals?

With the purpose

Of living my life

I feel so much alive,

I am here

To seek search

For my aim

Without wandering adrift

With no one to blame.

HOW TO BE SELF-DISCIPLINED?

Any person can develop self-discipline if he doesn't take liberty for granted. Discipline is doing what does not come naturally. It is hard, but it is the key to feeling in charge of your life. Self-discipline means adherence to the principle of doing the right thing rather than the instinctive thing and by the right thing it means that which is in your best interest in the long term. You have to have the self- disciplineto block out all the things that are not conducive to your growth andyour goals.

The ancient Chinese Philosopher, Mencius said, "Men must decide on what will not do and then they are able to act with vigour in what they ought to do".

You are the live remote who can access yourself to control you in your life. You are accountable for your actions. So if you acquire self-discipline you will lead your life to a great success all by yourself. In order to be self-disciplined you need to cease yourself from blaming others for your failures in life. Self-discipline can be formed through the habits you inculcate in you. This habit is not realised by us internally at the conscious level of our brain but it surfaces superficially in our subconcious mind. You may carry on your routine without any thought of what changes you need to acquire. In order to have self-discipline factor in your life, you need to notice where you fall short ofyour own faults.

In a nutshell, it means, "to know yourself" and "to know your limits".

"Self-discipline is the ability to make your self do what you should do, when you should do it, whether you feel like it or not.""

-Eibert Hubbard.

How to be self-disciplined?

To be self controlled

Is a disciplined manner indeed,

Life has so much to teach you

In every act or deed,

Do not waste time

Or take freedom for granted,

As liberty which you get

May turn you

To get yourself

A great success.

DISCOVERING THE TRUTH OF LIFE.

We all seek to search what is the truth of life by almost playing a wild-goose-chase. But this question about truth has an answer within itself that life is a biggest lie. For you to succeed you need to understand what's the living truth of passing a true life. Life in its moment is to live with a lie that you are living alive. But you aren't dead at the same time. To lead a successful life you shouldn't pass a sleep-living-life.

Now, the truth of life is to bookmark a mental note written by an anonymous author.

When you discover the life's purpose, embrace it with your entire being. You are unique in the entire universe. Goethe, a German writer and statesman who was a pictorial artist, biologist, theoretical physicist and polymath once said, "Man is not born to solve the problems of the universe, but to find out what he has to do".

Discover your life by discovering your own potential and there lies the truth of your success.

A living enlightened genius lives a most remarkable life. They understand the truth. The simple mindset of believing that you have the answers, lets your mind draw upon the universal store-house of knowledge. Napoleon Hill called it divine infinite intelligence. Religious-Science simply calls it Mind. Everything begins with a thought. Every answers to our life's questions have and always will be, inside of you and all around you. So look and hunt for it now! Trust yourself. You are a genius!

"If a man hasn't discovered something that he will die for, he isn't fit to live."

-Martin Luther King.

Discovering The Truth Of Life:

What is life?

Is it a child's play

To mould it like a clay?

What has it given?

What does it takes from us?

It is a mystery unsolved

It is a miracle unknown,

We feel our existence

And vanish from this earth

When our body departs soul

There will be nothing to hold,

So reason out the truth

Behind the given life,

Life is not a choice

Please act wise.

DISCOVER THE PERSON WITHIN YOU.

The secret of success lies when you know yourself. The self image which you carry shows who you are. The truth of discovering who you are leads you to first know yourself and then others. Life is a gift; It is the first and the last gift you will ever get.

Zig Ziglar, an American author, salesman, and motivational speaker says, "Most people are wandering generalities rather than meaningful specifics". Now, the very first step to know other people is to discover yourself! But our existence is yet to discover all throughout our living life till the day we die.

In the journey of your life a remarkable experience is to know, What do this adventurous word "I" means? Is it "I am a human creature, "I am a soul or spirit with presence of life within me", "I am a living proof of my own existence on this earth", "I am a dead person living a temporal life", "I am a person pursuing life-after- death in this world", or "I am alive by the wake of my soul's existence?"

Who am I? This truth is an unsolved mystery not yet known to you. You need not get perplexed with the dilemma you face in this situation. Create a new world with a new thought that "I am a person who is yet to discover who I am. Life teaches us a great lesson as we are all perpetual learners in this temporary class of worldly affairs setting forth the principles of who we are.

"When man first discovered the mirror, he began to lose his soul as he was concerned with his image more than that of his true self."

"Man's main task in life is to give birth to himself."

—*Erich Fromm.*

Discover The Person Within You:

Ever asked yourself

"Who are you?"

And failed to understand

Person within you?

Trace your talent

Explore it soon

So that you realize

What has life

To give you,

Believe in yourself

See the world

With your eyes

Do not shut it down

Until lord

Calls you upon.

FORECASTING YOUR FORTUNE.

According to Franklin Deleanor Roosevelt, an American statesman and political leader, "Men are not prisoners of fate; they are prisoners of their own mind."

Nothing on this earth is as powerful as you, to change the stars of your own destiny. Don't rely on predictions as if you predict, you lose the decision power which takes you into action mode in a negative manner.

If you control your future rather than the future controlling you then only you can make your presence felt. Your activity and your actions will definitely determine your fortune faithfully. To forecast your action or moment of life before-hand, will make you a failure as you missed out the very first step of your act. Be preplanned but do not forecast. Now, preplanning involves when you are making a plan priorly before you act in order to organise yourself well, whereas forecasting is merely a plan without action, predicting future and at the same time slaying your action for your achievement in life to be a successful person. Planning is a plan before act and forecasting is not to act after the plan. See what fortune has in store for you. You are endowed with all natural ways of leading your future life, forgetting and forgoing your past by filling your existence with your presence.

"Life is full of chances and changes and the most prosperous man may meet with misfortune."

-Aristortle.

Forecasting your fortune:

We are so unfortunate

That we blame luck

For failure at work,

And credit our efforts

For the life's purpose

Which we search,

To forecast

When future is not

In our hand,

Must not present

On this land!

SEEING BEYOND THE HORIZON.

In order to get the view of life with the clear vision of picturesque scenes of the outer world, you need to look what life has to offer you. Open the windows of your mind instead of shutting it down. Be open to new ideas and new concepts and the new opportunity will follow you one after another for your success. Stand back and look at your life from a higher plane or at a great distance.

It is said," Think Big and Do Big".

A person who limits himself to the boundaries created within him is paralyzed to analyze his success. Whereas if he crosses the limits looking what lies next beyond the horizon, he wins the victory with a long journey to reach himself to the world of great success.

"Freedom Is nothing else but a chance to be better"

-Albert Camus.

Seeing Beyond The Horizon:

When we see a mirage

We are almost under illusion

At our strongest vision,

Do not look at yourself

The way others look at you

In the zone of socialization

See beyond the horizon.

HOW TO LEARN FROM OUR MISTAKES.

As a human we all are imperfect. We are bound to make mistakes and learn from it. When you make mistakes you may not realize it was wrong what you did, but consequently you may face a situation which strikes you what went wrong and that is the first step of learning from your mistakes in life. We as humans are all perpetual learners in this world. Our brains are programmed and functioned to set a learning program.

Those who say "I'm right" or "I don't need to learn" have hampered their growth itself. They prove themselves that they are dead by the very fact they don't want to adopt new ideas, adapting to new changes, being open minded when it comes to learning lessons in life.

The former actress Joan Collins stated "Show me a person who has never made a mistake and I'll show you somebody who has never achieved much."

"Mistakes are a part of the dues one pays for a full life"

— By Sofia Loren.

How to learn from our mistakes?

When I was a toddler

In my early days,

I climbed up round and round

Every time I fell on the ground,

It was just a part of play

To learn to climb again and again

I was just such an insane

Then I was able to judge

How to walk even on road

Which is rough,

I crossed thousand miles

Where the hope for future arised.

HOW TO FACE REJECTION?

If you get rejected don't ever get dejected. Infact, get rejected till you aren't accepted. This is a "do-or-die" attitude which keeps you alive. What we perceive as bad-luck is nothing more than a blessing- in-disguise. When failure approaches you, you approach success. It will be a constant effort until you make your persistence die and it ceases to exist. If you win the race you will stay awake as alive and in this game you will win the victory of life.

Success itself is an eternal and integral part of life. It is in every moment that we can hear a faint voice whispering from deep inside our hearts, telling us that we were born to be successful. As a human being, it is our natural right to strive towards excellence and enjoy the fruits of achievement. This is the voice of intuition telling us that striving towards success is not suppose to be a drag, it is suppose to be a great delight. If you find that failure is your stagnation, all you need to do is work more hard to push you up. If you keep this feeling of stagnation being stoical about it to succeed in life, you will not be able to face the fact that you are rejected at all. Instead, take failure as an opportunity for you to climb the stairs by seizing success on the top inclined to see you as a winner, turning you out to be a successful person in life.

Do not belittle yourself. When rejection comes across, try to open the gate to welcome, but wave goodbye soon to it. It is because if rejection persists it should not demoralize you at the cost of your emotion and make you low in your spirits. Keep your inner self firm and confident. Face rejection and failures to rescue you as a last resort to be a great success rather than crying out a river for it. You need to cherish every moment of life.

Keep in your mind that, "In my rejection there is a process of acceptance which I imagine in reality, to make it real".

"In every adversity lies the seed of the equivalent or greater benefit".
-Napoleon Hill.

How to face rejection?

I was the one

Who got rejected

But never I got dejected,

For I am a creature

Made by lord's ingenious hands

Like an angel on this land,

As a human

I have self-respect at first,

I do not care

Even if my ego is hurt.

OPEN THE CLOSED DOOR, WALKING DOWN THE CORRIDOR.

The best way to arise when opportunity strikes to you is to make a start and begin your venture in the face of uncertainty. You should are to move forward taking a risk and embrace the unknown. It is said that action speaks more than words. When opportunity knocks on your door, don't let it go.

Try to make an effort reaching down the corridor where your ultimate success welcomes you. Cherish your failures and treasure your mistakes while you walk down. Do not look behind while walking towards the corridor as it becomes the matter of past which should not last with nostalgic impact. Look forward to make a future by working with your presence. You will find new doors opening for you when you move towards the success of life.

"When adversity strikes the easiest thing to do is quit, and that's exactly what the average man does."

-By Napoleon Hill.

Open the closed door,
walking down the corridor:

Time present

Is not to be found

In past or future,

For past

Can not come again,

For future

Is so much uncertain,

When you open

The closed door,

Walking down

The corridor

You reach your place

At the pace

Of a horse-rider!!!

YOUR PROBLEM IS YOUR PERSONAL GROWTH.

Trying to perceive your problems pessimistically will only aggravate it.

When a person leads a painful life throughout his age facing his ordeals, he tends to become more emotionally strong; as if he tries to seek solutions every time he is encountered with problems, then he becomes more experienced.

Solution lies in the problem itself.

So don't see your problem but seek a solution.

For instance, one cannot swim in the water without trying to root out the problem of fear of diving deep in it.

"Turn your wounds into wisdom"

-Oprah Winfrey.

Your Problem Is Your Personal Growth:

Without you permitting

A problem to exist,

The solution towards it

Will never arise,

To get accomplished

Problems are many more to say

It is like a child-play

Made of sand

Moulded as clay.

A SECOND TO MINUTE.

To lead the bright life you need to seize every moment to its fullest. Every day, every second, and every minute you breathe, you are living your timeless life which is quite infinite. Reap the seed! Follow an action! Live differently and Lead your life. Make a point to make a difference. Follow your own thought and in a friction of a second you self-analyse your mind. Remember that it takes a second to minute to change your moment. It is all in time and your action which leads to a moment of your life to deal with.

Harvey Mackay, an enterpreneur, motivational
speaker, author, and columnist says,
"Time is free,
But it's priceless.
You can't own it
But you can use it.
You can't keep it
But you can spend it.
Once you've lost it
You can never get it back".

"If you love life, don't waste time, for time is what life is made up of."
                                                                    -Bruce Lee

A Second to Minute:

When my life

Remains standstill

I stay in solitary moments

With my own will,

Life keeps changing

As time passes by

From a minute to a second

We fail to realize.

AUTHOR: SAMINA SAIFEE.

The author can be contacted for motivational or marriage counselling at her email id: saminasaifee2014@gmail.com

Inspired? Write A Poem!

Poem Title: _____ Date:
_____

_____

_____

_____

_____

_____

_____

_____

_____

_____

_____

_____

_____

_____

_____

_____

_____

_____

_____

Notes: _____

_____

_____

_____

Inspired? Write A Poem!

Poem Title: _____ Date: _____
_____

_____
_____
_____
_____

_____
_____
_____
_____

_____
_____
_____
_____

_____
_____
_____
_____

_____
_____
_____
_____

Notes: _____
_____
_____
_____

Inspired? Write A Poem!

Poem Title: _____ Date: _____
_____

_____
_____
_____
_____

_____
_____
_____
_____
_____

_____
_____
_____
_____

_____
_____
_____
_____

_____
_____
_____
_____

Notes: _____
_____
_____
_____

Inspired? Write A Poem!

Poem Title: _____ Date:
_____

_____
_____
_____
_____

_____
_____
_____
_____

_____
_____
_____
_____

_____
_____
_____

_____
_____
_____
_____

Notes: _____
_____
_____
_____

Inspired? Write A Poem!

Poem Title: _____ Date:
_____

_____

_____

_____

_____

_____

_____

_____

_____

_____

_____

_____

_____

_____

_____

_____

_____

_____

_____

Notes: _____

_____

_____

_____

Inspired? Write A Poem!

Poem Title: _____ Date:
_____

_____

_____

_____

_____

_____

_____

_____

_____

_____

_____

_____

_____

_____

_____

_____

_____

_____

_____

Notes: _____

_____

_____

_____

Inspired? Write A Poem!

Poem Title: _____ Date:

_____

_____

_____

_____

_____

_____

_____

_____

_____

_____

_____

_____

_____

_____

_____

_____

_____

_____

_____

_____

_____

_____

Notes: _____

_____

_____

_____

Inspired? Write A Poem!

Poem Title: _____ Date:

_____

_____
_____
_____
_____

_____
_____
_____
_____

_____
_____
_____
_____

_____
_____
_____
_____

_____
_____
_____
_____

Notes: _____
_____
_____
_____

Inspired? Write A Poem!

Poem Title: _____ Date:

_____

_____

_____

_____

_____

_____

_____

_____

_____

_____

_____

_____

_____

_____

_____

_____

_____

_____

_____

_____

_____

_____

Notes: _____

_____

_____

_____

Inspired? Write A Poem!

Poem Title: _____ Date:
_____

_____

_____

_____

_____

_____

_____

_____

_____

_____

_____

_____

_____

_____

_____

_____

_____

Notes: _____

_____

_____

_____

Inspired? Write A Poem!

Poem Title: _____ Date:
_____

_____

_____

_____

_____

_____

_____

_____

_____

_____

_____

_____

_____

_____

_____

_____

_____

_____

_____

Notes: _____

_____

_____

_____

Inspired? Write A Poem!

Poem Title: _____ Date:

_____

_____
_____
_____
_____

_____
_____
_____
_____

_____
_____
_____
_____

_____
_____
_____
_____

_____
_____
_____
_____

Notes: _____
_____
_____
_____

Inspired? Write A Poem!

Poem Title: _____ Date:

_____

_____

_____

_____

_____

_____

_____

_____

_____

_____

_____

_____

_____

_____

_____

_____

_____

_____

Notes: _____

_____

_____

_____

Inspired? Write A Poem!

Poem Title: _____ Date:
_____

_____
_____
_____
_____

_____
_____
_____
_____

_____
_____
_____

_____
_____
_____
_____

_____
_____
_____

Notes: _____
_____
_____
_____

Inspired? Write A Poem!

Poem Title: _____ Date:

_____

_____

_____

_____

_____

_____

_____

_____

_____

_____

_____

_____

_____

_____

_____

_____

_____

_____

_____

Notes: _____

_____

_____

_____

Inspired? Write A Poem!

Poem Title: _____ Date:
_____

_____
_____
_____
_____

_____
_____
_____
_____

_____
_____
_____
_____

_____
_____
_____
_____

_____
_____
_____

Notes: _____
_____
_____
_____

Inspired? Write A Poem!

Poem Title: _____ Date:

_____

_____

_____

_____

_____

_____

_____

_____

_____

_____

_____

_____

_____

_____

_____

_____

_____

_____

_____

_____

_____

Notes: _____

_____

_____

_____

Inspired? Write A Poem!

Poem Title: _____ Date:
_____

_____
_____
_____
_____

_____
_____
_____
_____

_____
_____
_____
_____

_____
_____
_____
_____

_____
_____
_____
_____

Notes: _____
_____
_____
_____

Inspired? Write A Poem!

Poem Title: _____ Date:

_____

_____

_____

_____

_____

_____

_____

_____

_____

_____

_____

_____

_____

_____

_____

_____

_____

_____

Notes: _____

_____

_____

_____

Inspired? Write A Poem!

Poem Title: _____ Date:
_____

_____
_____
_____
_____

_____
_____
_____
_____

_____
_____
_____
_____

_____
_____
_____
_____

_____
_____
_____
_____

Notes: _____
_____
_____
_____

Inspired? Write A Poem!

Poem Title: _____ Date: _____

_____

_____
_____
_____
_____

_____
_____
_____
_____
_____

_____
_____
_____
_____

_____
_____
_____
_____

_____
_____
_____
_____

Notes: _____
_____
_____
_____

Inspired? Write A Poem!

Poem Title: _____ Date:
_____

_____
_____
_____
_____

_____
_____
_____

_____
_____
_____
_____

_____
_____
_____

_____
_____
_____
_____

Notes: _____
_____
_____
_____

Inspired? Write A Poem!

Poem Title: _____ Date:
_____

_____
_____
_____
_____

_____
_____
_____
_____

_____
_____
_____
_____

_____
_____
_____
_____

_____
_____
_____
_____

Notes: _____
_____
_____
_____

Inspired? Write A Poem!

Poem Title: _____ Date:
_____

_____

_____

_____

_____

_____

_____

_____

_____

_____

_____

_____

_____

_____

_____

_____

_____

_____

_____

_____

_____

_____

_____

Notes: _____

_____

_____

_____

Inspired? Write A Poem!

Poem Title: _____ Date:

_____

_____

_____

_____

_____

_____

_____

_____

_____

_____

_____

_____

_____

_____

_____

_____

_____

_____

_____

_____

Notes: _____

_____

_____

_____

Inspired? Write A Poem!

Poem Title: _____ Date:

_____

_____

_____

_____

_____

_____

_____

_____

_____

_____

_____

_____

_____

_____

_____

_____

_____

_____

Notes: _____

_____

_____

_____

Inspired? Write A Poem!

Poem Title: _____ Date:

_____

_____

_____

_____

_____

_____

_____

_____

_____

_____

_____

_____

_____

_____

_____

_____

_____

_____

_____

_____

Notes: _____

_____

_____

_____

Inspired? Write A Poem!

Poem Title: _____ Date:
_____

_____
_____
_____
_____

_____
_____
_____
_____

_____
_____
_____

_____
_____
_____
_____

_____
_____
_____
_____

Notes: _____
_____
_____
_____

Inspired? Write A Poem!

Poem Title: _____ Date:

_____

_____

_____

_____

_____

_____

_____

_____

_____

_____

_____

_____

_____

_____

_____

_____

_____

_____

_____

Notes: _____

_____

_____

_____

Inspired? Write A Poem!

Poem Title: _____ Date:
_____

_____

_____

_____

_____

_____

_____

_____

_____

_____

_____

_____

_____

_____

_____

_____

_____

_____

Notes: _____

_____

_____

_____

Inspired? Write A Poem!

Poem Title: _____ Date:

_____

_____

_____

_____

_____

_____

_____

_____

_____

_____

_____

_____

_____

_____

_____

_____

_____

_____

_____

_____

_____

_____

Notes: _____

_____

_____

_____

Inspired? Write A Poem!

Poem Title: _____ Date:
_____

_____
_____
_____
_____

_____
_____
_____
_____

_____
_____
_____

_____
_____
_____

_____
_____
_____
_____

Notes: _____
_____
_____
_____

Inspired? Write A Poem!

Poem Title: _____ Date:

_____

_____

_____

_____

_____

_____

_____

_____

_____

_____

_____

_____

_____

_____

_____

_____

_____

_____

_____

_____

_____

_____

Notes: _____

_____

_____

_____

Inspired? Write A Poem!

Poem Title: _____ Date:
_____

_____
_____
_____
_____

_____
_____
_____
_____

_____
_____
_____
_____

_____
_____
_____

_____
_____
_____

Notes: _____
_____
_____
_____